Machinery 

Monitoring

A Practical Guide to Sampling and Analyzing Oil to Improve Equipment Reliability

By Mohammed Hamed Ahmed Soliman

ISBN-13: 979-8691140860

ASIN: B08K9XD22S

CONTENTS

CHAPTER 1
INTRODUCTION TO MAINTENANCE

Maintenance Policies and Strategies

Reliability centered maintenance promotes the use of Predictive and Risk Maintenance policies for identified critical equipment

Predictive Maintenance Techniques

Predictive Maintenance Embraced by Plant Maintenance

Technique	Application	Pumps	Electric Motors	Diesel Generators		Condensers	Heavy Equipment/ Crane	Circuit Breakers	Valves	Heat Exchangers	Electrical Systems	Transformers	Tank Piping
VIB Analysis		•	•	•			•						
Oil Analysis		•	•	•			•					•	
Wear Analysis		•	•	•			•						
IR Analysis		•	•	•	•	•	•	•	•	•	•	•	
Ultrasound		•	•	•	•			•	•	•	•	•	
Non-Destructive testing (Thickness)					•				•			•	
Visual Inspection		•	•	•	•	•	•	•	•	•	•	•	•
Motor Current Analysis			•										

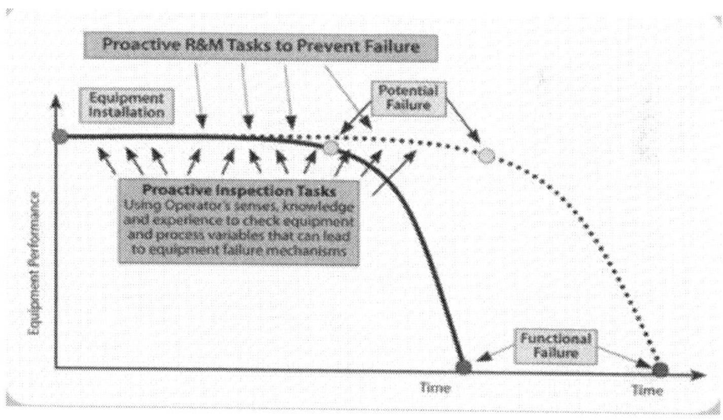

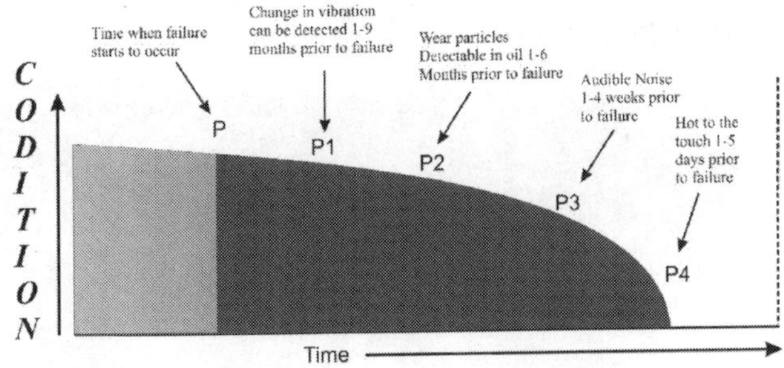
Time when failure starts to occur
Change in vibration can be detected 1-9 months prior to failure
Wear particles Detectable in oil 1-6 Months prior to failure
Audible Noise 1-4 weeks prior to failure
Hot to the touch 1-5 days prior to failure
P
P1
P2
P3
P4
CODITION
Time

Reliability KPIs

KPI	Description
MTBF	Mean Time Between Failure
No of failures addressed by root cause analysis	>75%
Ratio of PM work orders to CM work orders generated by PdM inspection	
OEE (Overall Equipment Effectiveness)	Availability x Reliability x Quality (85%)
Percent of Faults Found in Predictive maintenance Survey (Vib, IR, UT, OA)	No of faults found/ No of devices checked (target <3%
Percent of equipment covered by condition monitoring	Target= 100%
Reliability of critical equipment	99%
Facility Availability	>98%
Availability of critical equipment	>98%
Percent emergency maintenance	<5%
Percent planned maintenance	90%

Why Using Condition Monitoring Programs (Predictive Maintenance)?

Benefits of setting up a Predictive Maintenance (PdM) program:

1. To detect what is out of the human sense.
2. To discover hidden failures.
3. To detect early failures & monitor the machine health condition.
4. To reduce Maintenance Costs.
5. As a useful tool to improve the machine reliability.

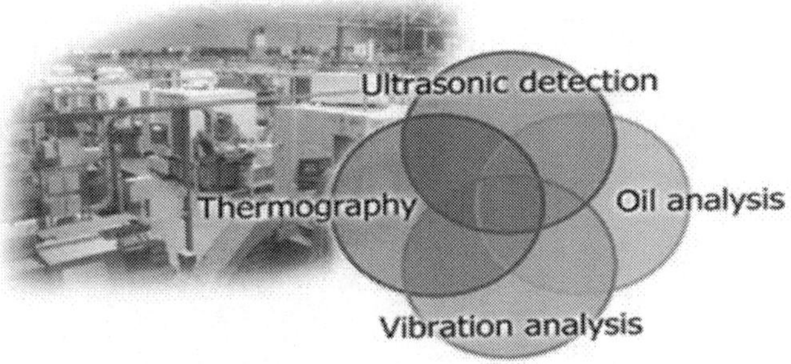

Four tools make up 85% of any PdM program

Infrared Thermography

Ultrasonic

Motor Current

Others eg.
Pressure Analysis,
Effeciency
Analysis

Oil

45%

Vibration Analysis

Vibration present 45% of PdM programs, oil present 15% but it can detect faults in equipment that vibration can't, e.g. electric transformers and hydraulic systems.

Equipment that fails in service can cost up to 10 times more to repair than the equipment repaired when predicted by condition monitoring.

Other PdM Techniques and Comparison

Notes:

Motor diagnosis = motor current analysis, and it's a technique involve intensive diagnosis of motor currents.

Oil Analysis involve Wear Particles Analysis for more intensive diagnosis about the sources of failure. For more information about the technique read the book: Machinery Oil Analysis and Condition Monitoring.

Thermography: involve thermal analysis using infrared camera. For more information about the technique, read the book: Industrial Applications of Infrared Thermography.

Ultrasound Analysis: is an acoustic method based on high frequencies measurement. For more information, read the book: Ultrasound Analysis for Condition Monitoring.

Why condition monitoring techniques?

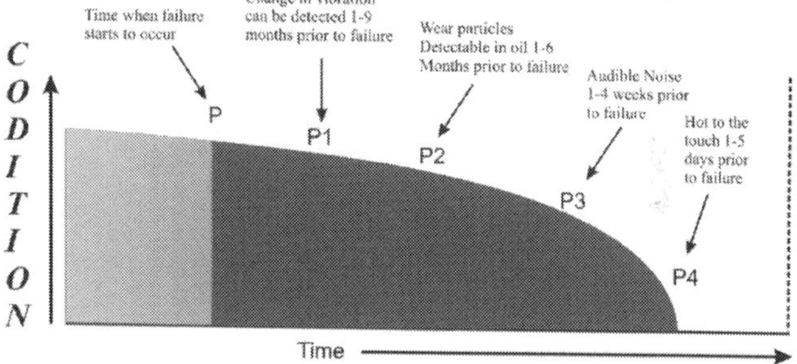

Vibration VS Thermography VS Oil Analysis

Type of fault	Vibration	Temp	Oil
Out of balance	XXX	----	----
Misalignment	XXX	X	----
Damage of bearing	XXX	XX	X
Damage of gear box	XXX	X	XX
Belt problems	XX	----	----
Motor problems	XX	X	----
Mechanical looseness	XXX	X	X
Resonance	XXX	----	----

While oil analysis can't detect various faults like vibration, but it's a less expensive technique, and doesn't require intensive training and practice like vibration.

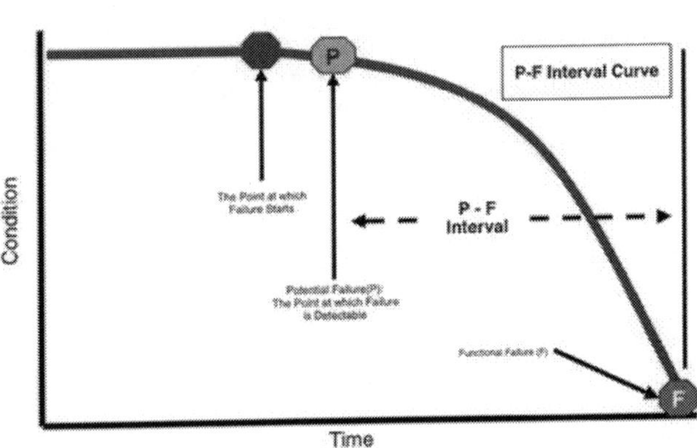

One of the most benefits of a condition monitoring program is to detect potential failures at early state.

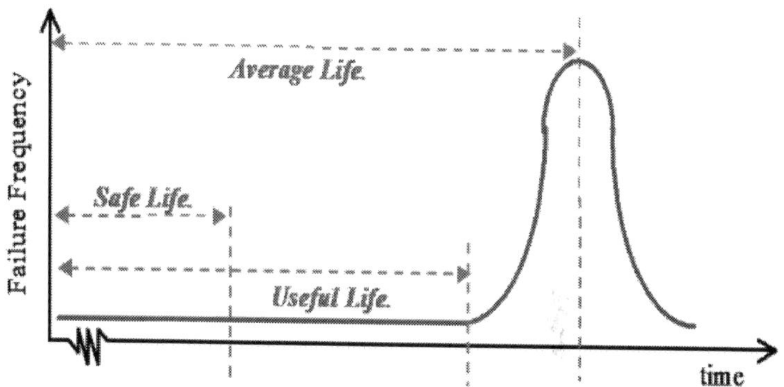

Determine the PM Interval Using Reliability Data from PdM Programs.

CHAPTER 2

INTRODUCTION TO OIL ANALYSIS DEFINITION AND PROCEDURES

Oil analysis involves sampling and analyzing oil for various properties and materials that indicate wear and contamination in an engine, transmission or hydraulic system.

Oil Analysis is the use of various laboratory tests to monitor lubricant health, equipment health and contamination.

Oil analysis (OA) is the sampling and laboratory analysis of a lubricant's properties, suspended contaminants, and wear debris. OA is performed during routine preventive maintenance to provide meaningful and accurate information on lubricant and machine condition.

Oil Analysis as a Part of Predictive Maintenance Programs PdM

Oil analysis technique utilize 15% of condition monitoring programs. Oil analysis is a long-term program that, where relevant, can eventually be more predictive than any of the other technologies. It can take years for a plant's oil program to reach this level of sophistication and effectiveness.

Analytical techniques performed on oil samples can be classified in two categories:

- Used Oil Analysis
- Wear Particles Analysis

Used oil analysis determines the condition of the lubricant itself, determines the quality of the lubricant, and checks its suitability for continued use. While **Wear Particles Analysis** determine the source of the wear by analyzing the metal contents. For example, spotting which sprocket inside gearbox is wearing.

Oil Analysis procedures

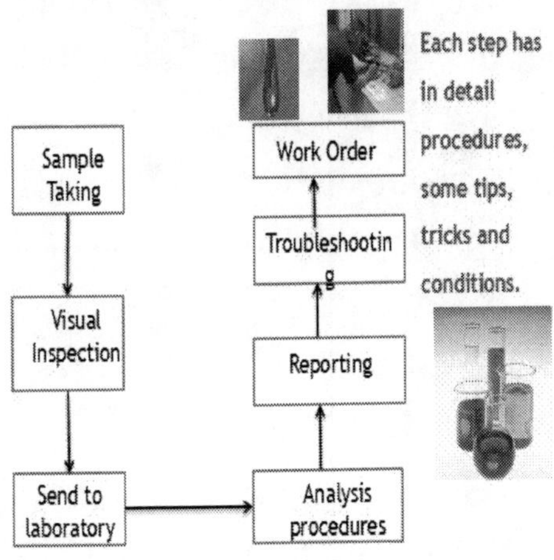

Terminologies Involve in Lubricant Systems

These terminologies will be used frequently in any oil analysis program or application.

Flash Point: the point at which the oil will

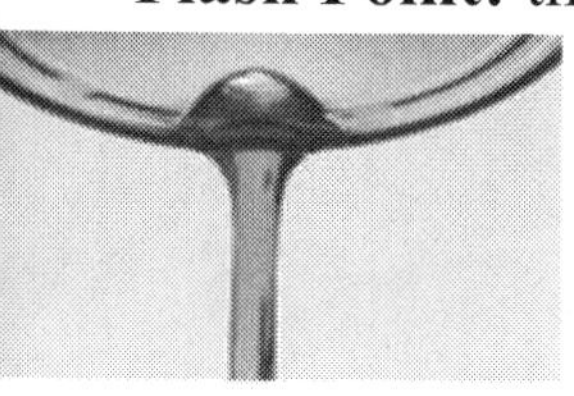

be turned into vapor or begin to vaporize.

Pour Point: the lowest temperature at which the oil will flow.

TBN: is the total base number, illustrate the no of he active additives left in the sample of oil to neutralize the acids. By comparing the TBN of a used oil to the TBN of the same oil in virgin condition, the user can determine how much reserve additive the oil has left to neutralize acids. The lower the TBN reading, the less active additive the oil has left.

The Viscosity Index is a measure of how much the oil's viscosity changes as temperature changes. A higher viscosity index indicates the viscosity changes less with temperature than a lower viscosity index.

TAN: is the total acid number, present how this oil is getting oxidized.

Role and Types of Different Oil Additives

Oil additives are chemical compounds that improve the lubricant performance of base oil. They vary from an oil to another based on the oil function. For example, car engine oil may contain viscosity modifiers to improve oil performance at different temperatures. While electric transformers oil may contain specific type of additives to improve oil insulation. It's really based on the oil function inside the equipment. Engine oils are used to protect from wears and tears. Transformer oils are used for isolation and cooling purposes. So what you basically look for in each oil type is totally different.

Detergent additives, dating back to the early 1930, are used to clean and neutralize oil impurities which would normally cause deposits (oil sludge) on vital engine parts.

Friction modifiers, like molybdenum disulfide, are used for increasing fuel economy by reducing friction between moving parts. Friction modifiers alter the lubricity of the base oil. While oil was used historically.

Anti-wear additives or wear inhibiting additives cause a film to surround metal parts, helping to keep them separated. Zinc Dialkyl Dithio Phosphate
(ZDDP) is a popular anti-wear additive, the use of which has been restricted thanks to potential damage to catalytic converters forced upon automakers by government regulation.

Pour point depressants improve the oil's ability to flow at lower temperatures.

Anti-foam agents inhibit the production of air bubbles and foam in the oil which can cause a loss of lubrication, pitting,
and corrosion where entrained air contacts metal surfaces.

Corrosion or rust inhibiting additives retard the oxidation of metal inside an engine.

Antioxidant additives retard the decomposition of the stock oil.

Viscosity modifiers make an oil's viscosity higher at elevated temperatures, improving its viscosity index (VI). This combats the tendency of the oil to become thin at high temperature. The advantage of using less viscous oil with a VI improver is that it will have improved low temperature fluidity as well as being viscous enough to lubricate at operating temperature. Most multi-grade oils have viscosity modifiers. Some synthetic oils are engineered to meet multi-grade specifications without them.

Seal conditioners cause gaskets and seals to swell so that the oil cannot leak by.

Metal deactivators create a film on metal surfaces to prevent the metal from causing the oil to be oxidized.

Extreme pressure agents bond to metal surfaces, keeping them from touching even at high pressure.

Dispersants keep contaminants (e.g. soot) suspended in the oil to prevent them from coagulating.

Wax crystal modifiers are DE waxing aids that improve the ability of oil filters to separate wax from oil. This type of additive has applications in the refining and transport of oil, but not for lubricant formulation.

Wear metals from friction are unintentional oil additives, but most large metal particles and impurities are removed in situ using either magnets or oil filters made for this purpose.

Most common elements found in the additives:

Barium (Ba), detergent or dispersant additive.

Boron (B), extreme-pressure additive.

Calcium (Ca), detergent or dispersant additive.

Copper (Cu), anti-wear additive.

Lead (Pb), anti-wear additive.

Magnesium (Mg), detergent or dispersant additive.

Molybdenum (Mo), friction modifier.

Phosphorus (P), corrosion inhibitor, anti-wear additive.

Silicon (Si), anti-foaming additive.

Sodium (Na), detergent or dispersant additive.

Zinc (Zn), anti-wear or anti-oxidant additive.

What can oil analysis tells you?

1. **Lubricant Health**

- Monitor changes in lubricant properties, determine the suitability for continued use:
- Additives metals analysis by ICP, Magnesium, Calcium, Silicon, Phosphorus, Zinc, Barium.
- Viscosity-Resistance to flow at temperature.
- Total Acid Number-Detect presence of acids.
- Total Base Number-Measure the ability to neutralize acids.

2. **Equipment Health**

- Detect ingression from external source.

- Is filter change required-high particles count.
- Is repair necessary-coolant leakage.

3. **Elemental analysis by Induction Couple plasma ICP**

- Water.
- Fuel Dilution.
- Soot.

4. **Determine effectiveness of maintenance strategy:**

- Reactive.
- Preventive.
- Predictive.

Basic Tests

Component Type	Elemental Analysis	Viscosity	Water	Acid NO	Oxidation	Particle Count
Engine	x	x	x		x	
Hydraulics	x	x	x	x	x	x
Gearbox	x	x	x	x	x	
Compressors	x	x	x	x	x	x
Turbines	x	x	x	x	x	x

Particle count is crucial to hydraulic systems, compressors, turbines, robotics and injection molding machines. When evaluating particle count data, particulate contamination has an immediate effect on the system. Clearance-size particles can cause slow response, spool jamming, surface erosion, solenoid burnout and may cause safety systems to fail.

Why TAN test shouldn't be used when sampling engine oils?

Engines produce carbon and other combustion components that will mix with oil and increase its acidity. Testing acidity in this case can be miss-leading. It's better to perform TBN to test how this oil is losing its basicity over time. There is a minimum level of TBN for each oil type.

CHAPTER 3

DIFFERENT TYPES OF OIL ELEMENTAL TESTS AND TECHNIQUES USED

Elemental Analysis by ICP (Inductively Coupled Plasma)

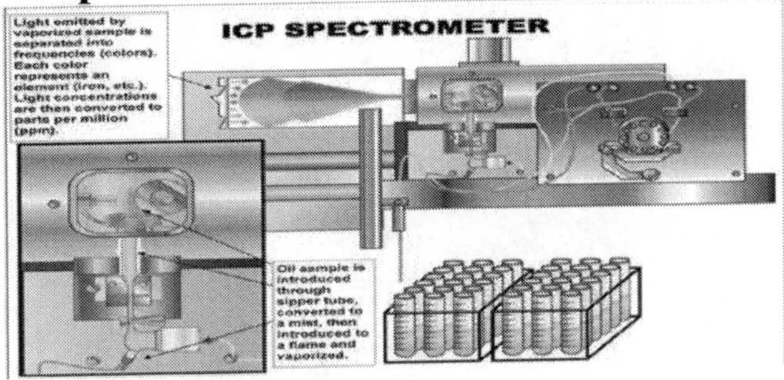

Test Methods: using a Rot rode Emission Spectrometer or an Inductively Coupled Plasma Spectrometer.

The Rot rode Spectrometer has a particle size detection limitation of between 3μ and 10μ (depending on the particular metal in question and the amount of surface oxidation on the particle surface) compared to the 0.5μ - 2μ limitation of the ICP.

Notice some metals can be both additives and contaminants, such as Calcium, or wear metals and additives, such as Zinc. The following table show so.

Elements are classified into:

Wear	Additives	Contaminant
Iron	Silicon	Silicon
Lead	Boron	Boron
Copper	Copper	Phosphorous
Tin	Sodium	Potassium
Aluminum	Phosphorous	Calcium
Chromium	Zinc	Magnesium
Nickel	Calcium	Vanadium
Silver	Magnesium	
Titanium	Molybdenum	
Antimony	Antimony	
Zinc	Potassium	

Viscosity Test

- ✓ Most important lubricant property (lubrication selection begins with viscosity calculation.
- ✓ Measure fluid resistance to flow under gravity.
- ✓ Relative to fluid density, thickness.
- ✓ Affects fluid ability to lubricate under different operating conditions.

Water Tests

Test is performed by several methods:

1. **Crackle**
   - ✓ Hot plate test, accurate up to 0.5%
   - ✓ Very subjective > 0.5%
   - ✓ Estimated.
2. **Karl Fischer ASTM D1744**
   Good test for turbine compressors, hydraulics, and some gear oils. Reported in % or ppm.
3. **Infrared**
   Fair accuracy unless contaminated with other.
   Factors: fuel, soot, glycol.
4. **Distillation**
   Very good test, usually cost prohibitive.

Water by Crackle %

Result is measured by placing a few drops of oil on a hot plate that is heated to 150° C. Positive water will bubble and crackle. Test is an estimate of % by volume and POLARIS Laboratories™ only reports an estimate up to 0.5%. The test is very subjective beyond 0.5%.

Test Limitation:
Accurate readings are difficult on emulsified fluids. Test is subjective and requires a minimum of 0.1% or 1000ppm to indicate a positive result. Should only be considered as a screening device for industrial hydraulics, gear boxes, compressors, bearing systems or turbines. Karl Fischer water should be performed on these unit types.

Oxidation Test

Oxidation measures the breakdown of a lubricant due to age and operating conditions. It prevents additives from performing properly, promotes the formation of acids and increases viscosity.

Nitration indicates excessive "blow-by" from cylinder walls and/or compression rings. It also indicates the presence of nitric acid, which speeds up oxidation. Too much disparity between oxidation and nitration can point to air to fuel ratio problems. As oxidation / nitration increases, so will total acid number and viscosity, while total base number will begin to decrease. Nitration is primarily a problem in natural gas engines.

Acid/Base Number Test

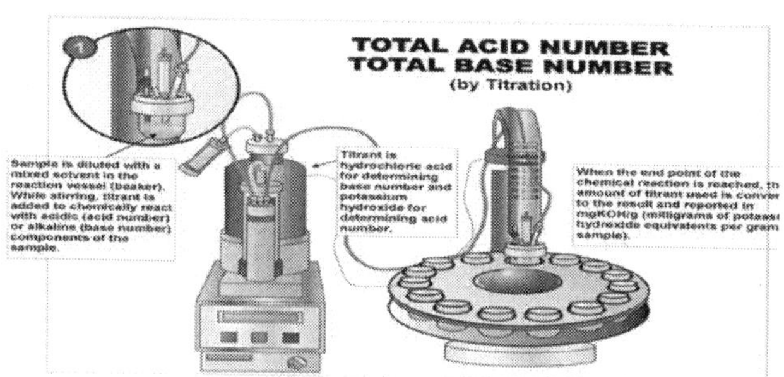

Oxidation is the most predominant reaction of a lubricant in service. It is responsible for numerous lubricant problems including:

- ✓ Viscosity increase.
- ✓ Varnish, sludge and sediment formation.
- ✓ Additive depletion.
- ✓ Base oil breakdown.
- ✓ Filter plugging.
- ✓ Loss in foam control.
- ✓ Acid number (TAN) increase.
- ✓ Rust formation and corrosion.

Oxidation is always an indication of the oil age when compared to the new oil.

Particle Quantifier (Ferrous Density) exposes a lubricant to a magnetic field. The presence of any ferrous metal causes a distortion in the field, which is represented as the PQ Index, an arbitrary unit of measurement that correlates well with DR Ferro large. Although PQ does not provide a ratio of small to large ferrous particles, if the PQ Index is smaller than iron parts per million (ppm) by ICP, it's unlikely there are any particles larger than 10 microns present. If the PQ Index increases dramatically while the ICPs iron parts per million (ppm) remains consistent or goes down, larger ferrous particles are being generated. Analytical Ferrography should then be used to qualify the type of wear occurring.

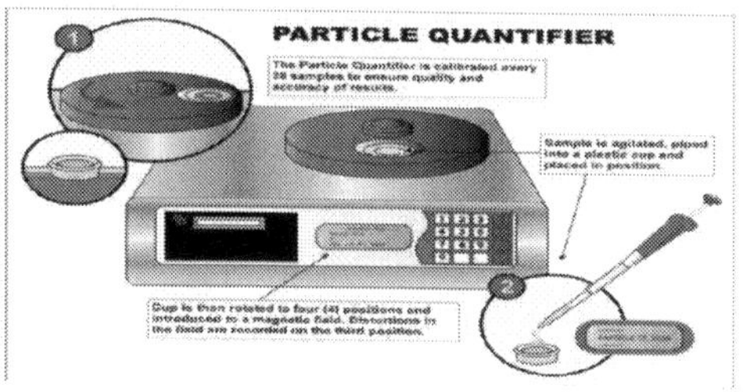

Wear Particle Analysis

Determines the mechanical condition of machine components that are lubricated. Eg. This test allows identifying which sprocket or gear tooth are faulty inside a gearbox by analyzing metal contents to identify where the failure is coming from.

Aluminum	Pistons, bearings, pumps, thrust washers
Antimony	Bearings, grease
Barium	Rust and oxidation inhibitor additives, grease
Boron	Anti-corrosion additives in coolant, dust, water
Calcium	Detergent/dispersant additives
Chromium	Piston rings in internal combustion engines
Copper	Bearings, brass/bronze alloys, bushings, thrust washers
Iron	Shafts, rolling-element bearings, cylinders, gears, piston rings
Lead	Bearings, fuel additives, anti-wear additives
Lithium	Grease, additives
Magnesium	Transmissions, detergent additives
Molybdenum	Piston rings, electric motors, extreme-pressure additives
Nickel	Bearings, valve train, turbine blades
Phosphorus	Anti-wear additives, extreme-pressure gear additives
Potassium	Coolant additives
Silver	Bearing cages (plating), gear teeth, shafts
Silicon	Dust/dirt, defoamant additives
Sodium	Detergent or coolant additives
Tin	Journal bearings, bearing cages, solder

Measuring should be in trends, excess wears can lead to breakdowns.

Oil Analysis:

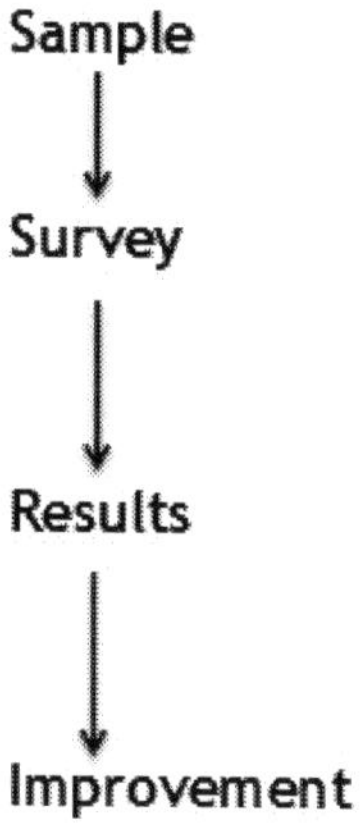

CHAPTER 4
CASE STUDY: ANALYZING ENGINE OIL

Overview

Oil properties vary based on the equipment its being used in, and its function in this equipment. What you measure is the functional failure of this oil. For example, in engines, the main function of oil is to protect against wear, corrosion, and high temp working condition. Oil in engines is stressed by the pressure of pistons. Therefore, it's very important to measure acidity/base number, viscosity, and flash point to determine how the oil has been degraded and if there is any wear has occurred. Also measuring water in oil is useful to determine if there is a leakage in the system.

Data Required To Perform Engine Oil Analysis

Oil Grade: Eg. 0W-40, 5W-30

Oil Type:
Equipment Type:
Oil Specifications:
Viscosity@40degC
Viscosity@100degC
Total Base Number (TBN)
Total Acid Number (TAN)
Flash Point
Oil Manufacturer: Asmoil
Oil Grade : Synthetic Motor Oil SAE 5W-30
Oil type : Engine Oil
Filter type : Full Flow

Oil Analysis Report:

Parameters	Standard acc to SAE for engine grade 30	1-1-2009	1-1-2010
Viscosity@40C	90-110cSt	100	98
Viscoisty@100C	9.3-12.5cSt	11.5	8.6
Fuel Content %	0	0	5
Water Content %	0	0	2
TAN	--------	-----------	----------
TBN	6-8	7	3.82
Flash Point rate for Asmoil 5W-30 grade	375°F<	385	375

Rermark: cSt=Centi Stoke

Parameters	Standard acc to SAE for engine grade 30	1-1-2009	1-1-2010
Viscosity@40C	90-110	100	98
Viscoisty@100C	9.3-12.5	11.5	8.6
Fuel Content %	0	0	5
Water Content %	0	0	2
TAN	--------	-----------	----------
TBN	6-8	7	3.82
Flash Point rate for Asmoil 5W-30 grade	375°F<	385	375

➢Green color indicate good condition, yellow color indicate alarm level, red color indicate that oil must be changed.

Recommendations based on the result:

- Viscosity has been broken down at 100degC, oil should be changed due to reduction in viscosity index number which will reduce the friction resistivity of the oil.
- Oil is contamination with fuel indicating leakage in the piston rings.
- Oil has water contents indicating failure head gasket or worn cylinder head, check for compression ratio of your engine.
- TBN is below the oil standard, this indicate wear, oil must be changed.
- Flash point is below the oil number, oil can be vaporized easily.

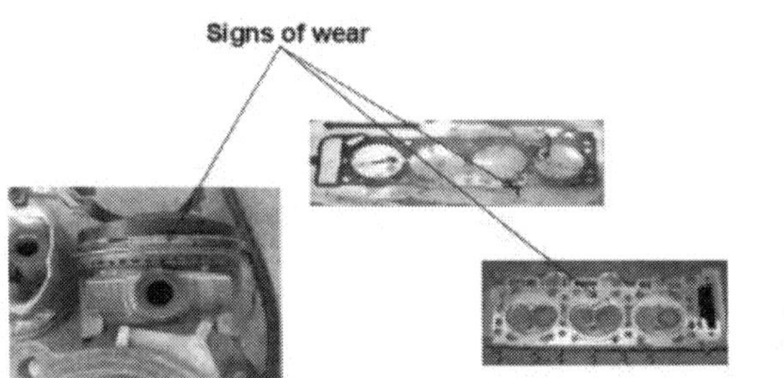

A wear in the head gasket or cylinder head can cause leakage of water to the oil system, degrading oil, reducing its ability to protect the pistons and the other mechanical parts against wear. An overtime wear in the piston itself or the piston ring will appear in the oil analysis results. But you can determine which part is wearing (piston or piston ring) by performing a wear particles analysis test.

It's important to understand that we don't measure oil properties to only change oil! But to realize the equipment condition and determine what parts need to be considered for changing, what action to take and what type of failure is going to happen. E.g. a slight wear in the piston rings can be early detected and those rings can be changed before a bigger failure occur! A worn piston rings can damage the pistons, worse the cylinder itself! Result in huge costs for engine re building.

Wear particles analysis test is very useful to determine where the wear is coming from. It can be the piston rings, valves, valves seals, pistons, or the cylinder.

CHAPTER 5
SAMPLING METHODS

The frequency of sample analysis from your equipment depends on the machine type, machine application and condition, operating environment and other variables. For example, many machines that operate in harsh environments, such as heavy equipment in mining or construction, require short oil sampling intervals - every 100 to 300 operating hours.

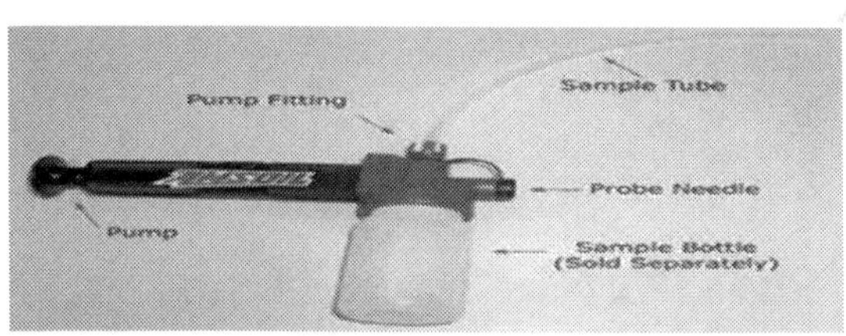

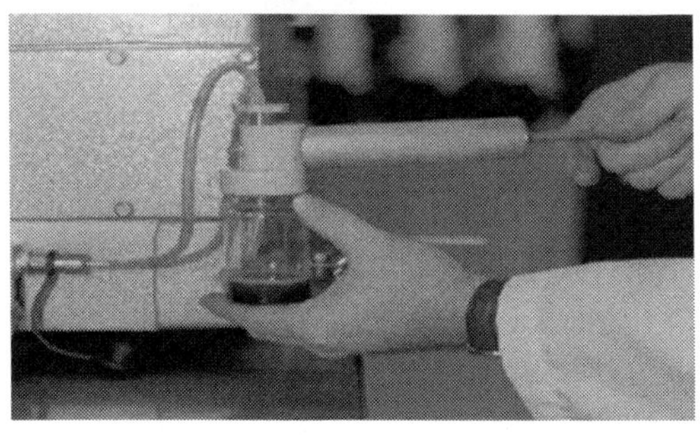

Oil sample taken can be sent to the laboratory for testing or to be tested on field using a special analyzer.

Results reported in 2 to 4 days after the lab receives the sample.

Benefits of Oil Analysis:

- ✓ Indicate how the equipment was used.
- ✓ Illustrate what condition equipment is in.
- ✓ Indicate the presence of contaminants.
- ✓ Tell if you are using the proper lubricant.

Targets from the Oil Analysis Program:

- ✓ Eliminating too-frequent oil changes.
- ✓ Reduce the cost for oil and servicing.
- ✓ Detect hidden wears.
- ✓ Detect machine health condition& evaluate it.
- ✓ Determine root causes of failures.

CHAPTER 6
VIBRATION VS OIL ANALYSIS

Vibration VS Oil Analysis

Condition	Oil program	Vibration program	Correlation
Water in oil	Strong	Not applicable	Water can lead to a rapid failure. It is unlikely that a random monthly vibration scan would detect the abnormality.
Greased bearings	Mixed	Strong	It makes economic sense to rely on vibration monitoring for routine greased bearing analysis. Many lube labs do not have enough experience with greased bearings to provide reliable Information.
Greased motors-operated valves	Mixed	Weak	Actuators are important machinery in the nuclear industry. Grease samples can be readily tested, but it can be difficult to obtain a representative sample. It can be hard to find these valves operating, making it difficult to monitor with vibration Techniques.
Shaft cracks	Not applicable	Strong	Vibration analysis can be very Strong effective to monitor a cracked Shaft.

Condition	Oil program	Vibration program	Correlation
Lubricant condition monitoring	Strong	Not applicable	The lubricant can be a significant cause of failure.
Resonace	Not applicable	Strong	Vibration program can detect a resonance condition. Lube analysis will eventually see the effect.
Root Cause Failure Analysis	Strong	Strong	Best when both programs work together.

Condition	Oil program	Vibration program	Correlation
Gear wears	Strong	Strong	Vibration techniques can link a defect to a particular gear. Lube analysis can predict the type of failure mode.
Alignment	Not applicable	Strong	Vibration program can detect a misalignment condition. Lube analysis will eventually see the effect of increased/improper bearing load.

Oil Analysis Can be used with anything use oil such as:

- ✓ All gearboxes for (trucks, cars, stirrers, turbines, industrial equipment…etc.)
- ✓ All engines that use oil (cars, trucks, heavy equipment…etc.)
- ✓ All hydraulic systems.

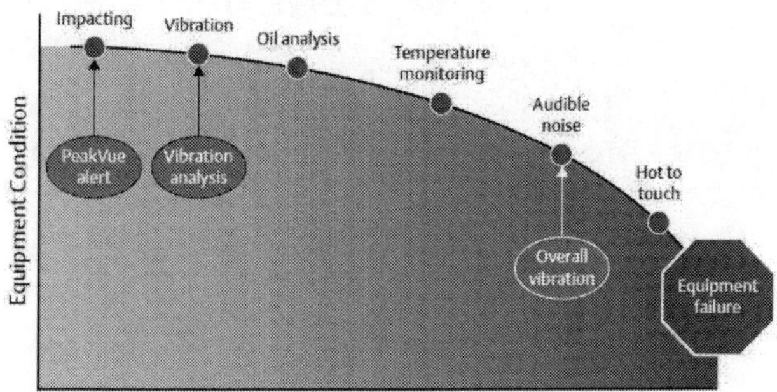
Impacting
Vibration
Oil analysis
Temperature monitoring
Audible noise
Hot to touch
PeakVue alert
Vibration analysis
Overall vibration
Equipment failure
Equipment Condition
Time

CHAPTER 7
CASE STUDY: TURBINE OIL CONDITION MONITORING

Types of tests performed on turbines according to the American Society for Testing Materials

Viscosity ASTM D445

Viscosity is the most important property of any lubricant.

Viscosity is defined as the resistance to flow of oil at a given temperature and is measured via the ATSM D445 protocol. As it relates to turbine oils, significant changes to viscosity usually indicate that the oil has become contaminated with another oil. In very severe cases, viscosity will increase as a result of excessive oxidation. Thermal cracking (from excessive heat) of the base oil can cause the viscosity to decrease.

Oxidation Stability by Rotary Pressure Vessel

Oxidation Test (ASTM D2272)

Rotary Pressure Vessel Oxidation Test (RPVOT and formerly known as RBOT) is a measure of remaining oxidation life when compared to new oil. The test is not intended to draw comparisons between two different new oils or oils of different chemistries. In fact, oils with very high new oil RPVOT values have been seen to have the short test life in laboratory rig testing. ASTM D4378 defines 25 percent of the new oil RPVOT value as the lower limit. When the oil is approaching the 25 percent of new oil value in conjunction with an increasing TAN, ASTM D4378 recommends that plans should be made to replace the charge of oil.

Total Acid Number (ASTM D974)

Total Acid Number (TAN) is the measure of the oil's acidity and is measured by titrating the oil with a base material (KOH) and determining the amount of base required to neutralize the acids in the oil. The results are reported as mg KOH/g of the oil being tested.

TAN measures the acidic by products formed during the oxidation process. ASTM D4378 (In Service Monitoring of Mineral Turbine Oils for Steam and Gas Turbines) recommends that a 0.3 to 0.4 mg KOH/g rise above the new oil value as the warning limit. Any significant change in TAN should be investigated as the acids in the oil can cause corrosion of bearing surfaces that result in irreparable damage. However, care should be taken in reacting to a single high TAN result. The TAN test is not a precise method (+/- 40 percent by ASTM Standard) and is subject to variability of operators. Poor maintenance of the buffer solution or electrodes used in the titration can also yield false results.

Foam Tendency and Stability (D892, Sequence I)

The presence of some foam in the reservoir is normal and not a cause for concern. Excessive foaming is generally not related to the oil, but rather to mechanical issues that cause excessive amounts of air to be introduced to the oil. Contamination and oil oxidation can also have an effect on the foaming tendency and stability. Excessive amounts of foam are a concern to the turbine operator for two reasons:

First is a safety and housekeeping issue if the foam overflows the reservoir. Second, excessive amounts of air in the oil can lead to more rapid oxidation and a phenomenon known as micro-dieseling. Micro-dieseling is caused when an air bubble in the oil is rapidly and adiabatically compressed causing extreme local temperature increases. These large temperature increases are known to cause thermal and oxidative degradation of the oil leading to deposit formation.

ASTM D4378 offers the guideline of 450 ml of foaming tendency and 10 ml of stability in Sequence I test.

Colorimetric Analysis

Colorimetric analysis is designed to measure the insoluble materials in the turbine oil which often lead to varnish deposits. The process includes treating the lubricant sample with a specific chemical mixture designed to isolate and agglomerate insoluble by-product material, and collect this material on a filter patch. The color spectra of the collected material is then evaluated and depending on the intensity of specific colors or color ranges, a varnish potential rating may be derived. The filter patch may also be weighed as a means to determine insoluble concentration in the lubricant. Several commercial labs utilize this technique, each with their own specific method.

Currently, this is not covered by an ASTM standard, but an ASTM method is currently being developed based on this concept.

The color of every object we see is determined by a process of absorption and emission of the electromagnetic radiation (light) of its molecules. Colorimetric analysis is based on the principle that many substances react with each other and form a color which can indicate the concentration of the substance to be measured. When a substance is exposed to a beam of light of intensity I0 a portion of the radiation is absorbed by the substance's molecules, and a radiation of intensity I lower than I0 is emitted.

Contamination Measurement

Water Content – (Visual and ASTM D1744)

Turbine oils are subject to water contamination from several sources. Steam turbines can have leaking gland seals or steam joints. All turbines can become contaminated with water from atmospheric condensation in the reservoir or leaking heat exchangers. The turbine oil should be inspected daily for water. Looking at the sample, it should be clear and bright. A cloudy or hazy appearance indicates that water may be present. An on-site water test can be performed such as the hot plate crackle test where the subject oil is dropped on a heated metal surface. Bubbling and crackling indicate that water is present. In the laboratory, water is typically measured by Karl Fischer Titration (ASTM D1744) and reported as a percent or in parts per million.

ASTM D4378 identifies 1,000 ppm or 0.1 percent water as a warning limit. However, some OEM's have defined 500 ppm as the warning limit. Keep in mind that the Karl Fisher method does not measure free water, so daily visual inspections of the turbine oil are recommended.

Metals by Inductively Coupled Plasma (ICP)

Metals concentration in a turbine oil can give early warning of wear conditions, changes in equipment operation or potential contamination issues. Keep in mind however, that the size of the metals detected by this method is limited to very small metal particles, typically less than 8 microns in size. That means catastrophic failures can occur where large pieces of wear metal are generated and not detected by this test. There is no specific limit on the amount of metals for turbine oils. The trend of metals concentration is often the most important aspect of this test.

Ultra Centrifuge Rating

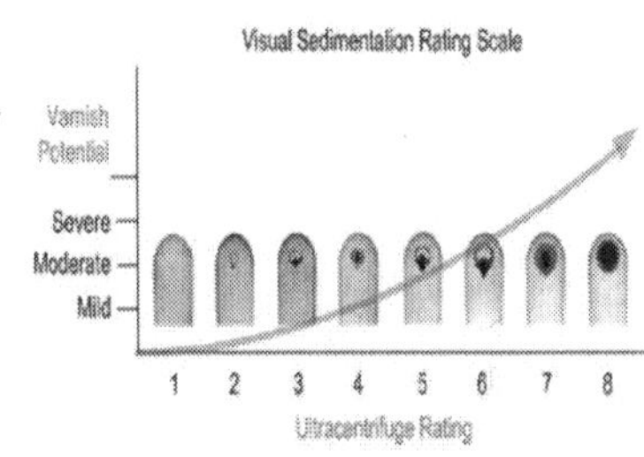

The Ultra Centrifuge test detects finely dispersed or suspended particles in the oil. The subject oil sample is centrifuged at 17,500rpm for 30 minutes. At the end of this period, the test tube is drained and the remaining sediment is rated.

Particle Count (ISO 4406)

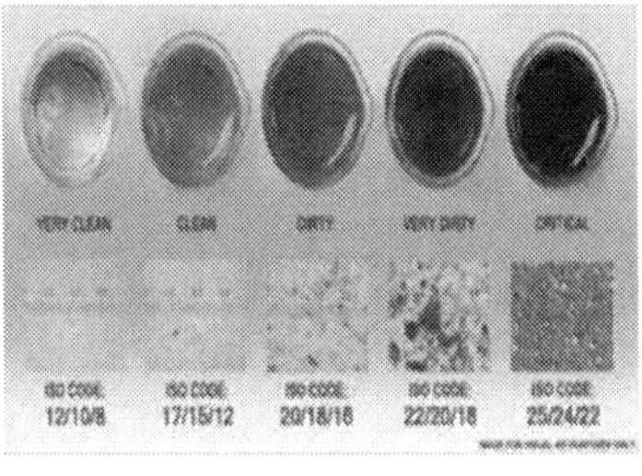

Particle Counting and ISO Cleanliness ratings define the concentration of particles in the oil and relate this back to the ISO Cleanliness scale. The results are reported as the number of particles greater than 4 microns/6 microns/ 14 microns per ml of fluid. The ISO Cleanliness Code relates the number of particles per ml to a logarithmic scale with code number for each range. A typical result would look like

18/16/13 where 18 means there is 1,300 to 2,500 particles per ml greater than 4 microns in size, 320 to 640 greater than or equal to 6 microns, and 40 to 80 greater than 14 microns.

Particle counts are subject to a wide range of variability due to sample preparation, oil formulations, contamination of the sample container, and location and method of sampling. There are also differences in the equipment used to measure particle counts between light dispersion techniques and filter pore blockage methods. Care should be taken to ensure that the samples used for Particle Counts are representative and consistent. The particle count results are only good as a relative measure of contamination and no ASTM standard exists for this test. Ultimately, particle count does give a good indication of overall system cleanliness. OEMs do offer some guidelines for new and used oils, but in general an ISO Cleanliness code of 18/15/13 or lower is an acceptable result.

Performance Properties Test

Demulsibility (ASTM D1401)

Demulsibility is a measure of the oil's ability to separate from water. The 40 ml of the subject oil and 40 ml of distilled water are mixed and then allowed to settle. The amount of time for full separation of the oil and water is recorded or after 30 minutes, the amounts of oil water and emulsion are recorded. ASTM does not offer a warning limit for demulsibility, but a result of 15 ml or greater of emulsion after 30 minutes is a fair warning limit. Contamination and oil age are factors that negatively affect demulsibility. Care should be taken when evaluating demulsibility as the preparation of the glassware and the quality of the water used can yield false or failing results.

Suggested Oil Analysis Schedule for Turbine System

Test	Steam	Gas	Frequency
Viscosity-ASTM D445	x	x	Monthly
TAN- ASTM D664	x	x	Monthly
RPVOT (oxidation test) - ASTM D2272	x	x	Quarterly
Water content (visual)	x	x	Daily
Water content-ASTM D1744	x	x	Monthly
Particle count	x	x	Monthly
Rust test	x	x	Only if corrosion issue
Foam	x	x	Only if foam is an issue
Demulsibility	x	x	Only if water separation is concern
Ultra centrifuge	x	x	Monthly to Quarterly
Varnish potential rating		x	Monthly to Quarterly

Troubleshooting the Oil Analysis Result for Turbine

Low Viscosity	High Viscosity	TAN	Metals	Particle Count	Water
Low viscosity oil used as make-up	Higher viscosity oil used as make-up	Increasing or high oxidation	Inaccurate sample (bottom sample)	Inaccurate sample	Atmospheric condensation
Mechanical shear in VI improved oils	Excessive oxidation	Wrong oil	Component wear		Leaking oil coolers
Contamination with solvents	Hot spots within the system	Contamination with a different fluid	Wrong oil	Filtration equipment not operating properly	Ingress of water wash

Low Viscosity	High Viscosity	TAN	Metals	Particle Count	Water
Thermal cracking from excessive heat (such as electric tank heaters)	Over extended oil drain interval	Testing variability	Sealants	Poor storage and handling procedures	Steam leaks
Bad or mis-labeled sample	Contamination		Thread compounds		Poor oil demulsibility

Low Viscosity	High Viscosity	TAN	Metals	Particle Count	Water
	Bad or miss-labeled sample		Contaminants		Oil conditioning equipment not functioning properly
			Assembly lubes		Inaccurate sample (bottom samples)

CHAPTER 8
CASE STUDY: OIL CONDITION MONITORING FOR ELECTRICAL COMPONENTS

Overview

Oil being used in electrical components such as transformers (those types of transformers immersed in oil) has different function and properties. What you measure depend on the oil function, because you usually measure functional failures. For exampl, the oil function inside a transformer is the isolation and cooling. Therefore, you should measure the inslulation ability of the oil and its capability to resist electric breakage. Measuring water in oil is not to detect leakage (unlike in engines) but to determine if there is excess moisture that will prevent the oil from doing its job in isolation.

Test	Standard ASTM Reference
Dielectric Breakdown Voltage, KV	D877 D1816
Water Content, Maximum PPM	D1533
Power Factor, %	D924
Interfacial Tension, dynes/cm	D971 D2285
Acidity, mgKOH/gm	D974

According to the American Society for Testing Materials

1. Dielectric Breakdown:

The dielectric breakdown voltage is a measurement of electrical stress that an insulating oil can withstand without failure.

2. Power Factor:

The power factor of insulating oil equals the cosine of the phase angle between an ac voltage applied and the resulting current. Power factor indicates the dielectric loss of the insulating oil and, thus, its dielectric heating.

3. Interfacial Tension

The interfacial tension (IFT) test is employed as an indication of the sledging characteristics of power transformer insulating oil. It is a test of IFT of water against oil.

4. Water Content

Actual water percentage exist in the oil sample.

Gas Dissolved Tests (according to ASTM standard)

Gases		Allowed percentage in 11KV Transformer
Acethylene1	C_2H_2	From Oil Table depend on the oil type used.
Nitrogen	N_2	
Carbon monoxide1	CO	
Oxygen	O_2	
Methane1	CH_4	
Carbon Dioxide	CO_2	
Ethane1	C_2H_6	
Ethylene1	C_2H_4	
Hydrogen1	H_2	

Troubleshooting Dissolved Gas Analysis (Example)

Gas	Normal	Abnormal	Problem
H_2	<150 ppm	>1000 ppm	Corona, Arcing
CH_4	<25 ppm	>80 ppm	Sparking
CO	<500 ppm	>1000 ppm	Severe Overloading
CO_2	<10000 ppm	>150000 ppm	
C_2H_4	<20 ppm	>100 ppm	Severe Overheating
C_2H_6	<10 ppm	>35 ppm	
C_2H_2	<15 ppm	>70 ppm	Arcing

Oil Analysis Interval for Transformers

Rating	Type of Transformer	Period Between Testing (months)	
		Gas	Oil
>1MVA	Furnace (critical)	3	6-12
	Distribution	6	6-12
	Special	3-6	6-12
<1MVA	Any type	6-12	12

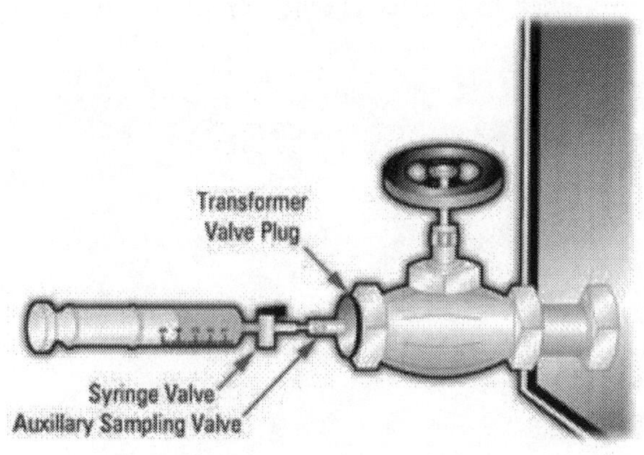

Sampling oil method from a transformer.

Oil sampling technique requires training.

CHAPTER 9
OIL MONITORING SYSTEMS AND DEVICES

Portable Oil Analyzer

Applications: All types of engines include car, trucks, loaders, turbines, and generators.

Quick indication for:

- ✓ TAN.
- ✓ TBN.
- ✓ Oxidation degree.

Water in oil portable analyzer

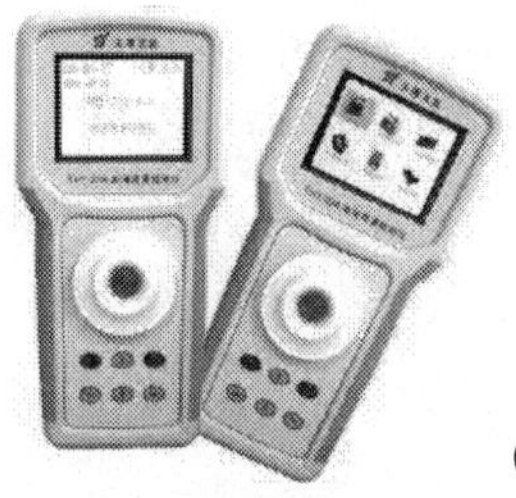

Oil quality analyzers

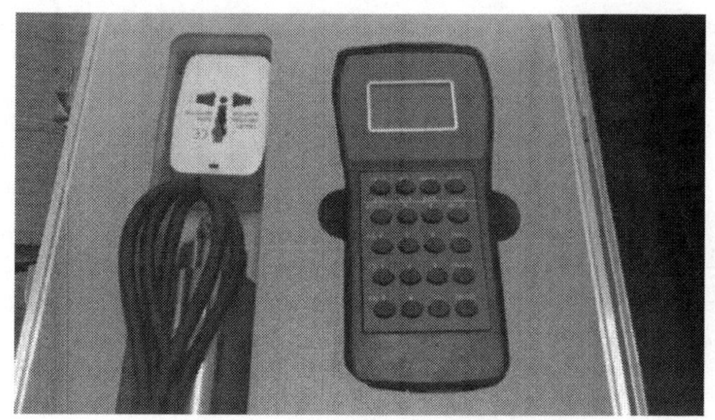

Oil contaminations analyzer

Online Oil Condition Monitoring
Online oil condition checking gives bits of knowledge into oil degradation over the long run, distinguishing denouncing limits, ascertaining oil RUL, and quick identification of contamination occasions.

Benefits:

- ✓ Continuous oil wellbeing data takes into consideration, result in better allocation of resources.
- ✓ More exact information lessens pointless spare parts costs through preventive maintenance furthermore, broadening oil RUL.
- ✓ Early admonition of potential failure modes permits for better end of-life administration.
- ✓ Continuous web based observing lessens breakdowns and emergency maintenance.

Instruments used:

- Wear debris sensors.
- Online oil condition-based sensors.
- Multi-sensor systems.

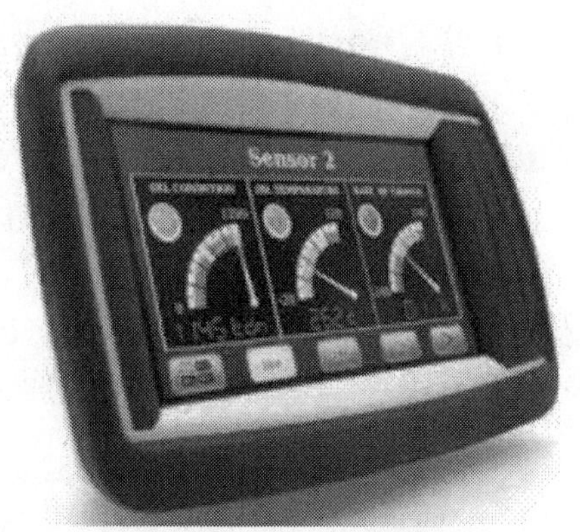

Online Oil Monitoring.

Oil Condition Based Oil System Should be used for Critical Components.

Online Condition Based Oil Monitoring is Ideal for:

- Oil Machineries.
- Motor and Pumps Bearings.
- Diesel and Gas Engines.

- Air and Gas Compressors.
- Chillers and Refrigeration.
- Transmission and Final Drive. Differentiations.
- Industrial Gas Oils.
- Steam Turbines.
- Gas Turbines.
- Hydraulic Systems.

REFERENCES

Noria Oil Sampling Procedures. Noria Corporation.

Scheffer, C. and Girdhar, P. 2004. Practical Machinery Vibration Analysis and Predictive Maintenance: Newnes; 1st Edition Predictive.

Oil Analysis Basics: Second Edition. Noria Corporation.

Scheffer, C. and Girdhar, P. 2004. Practical Machinery Vibration Analysis and Predictive Maintenance: Newnes; 1st Edition Predictive.

Soliman, M. H. A. 2020. Vibration Basics and Machine Reliability Simplified: A Practical Guide to Vibration Analysis.

Soliman, M. H. A. 2020. Machine Reliability and Condition Monitoring: A Comprehensive Guide to Predictive Maintenance Planning.

Soliman, M. H. A. 2020. Overall Equipment Effectiveness Simplified: Analyzing OEE to Find the Improvement Opportunities.

Soliman, M. H. A. 2014. Analyzing Failure to Prevent Problems. Industrial Management 56 (5), 10.

ABOUT THE AUTHOR

Mohammed Hamed Ahmed Soliman is an industrial engineer, consultant, university lecturer, operational excellence leader, and author. He works as a lecturer at the American University in Cairo and as a consultant for several international industrial organizations.

Soliman earned a bachelor of science in Engineering and a master's degree in Quality Management. He earned post-graduate degrees in Industrial Engineering and Engineering Management. He holds numerous certificates in management, industry, quality, and cost engineering.

For most of his career, Soliman worked as a regular employee for various industrial sectors. This included crystal-glass making, fertilizers, and chemicals. He did this while educating people about the culture of continuous improvement.

Soliman has lectured at Princess Noura University and trained the maintenance team in Vale Oman Pelletizing Company. He has been lecturing at The American University in Cairo for 6 year and has designed and delivered 40 leadership and technical skills enhancement training modules.

Soliman is a member at the Institute of Industrial and Systems Engineers and a member with the Society for Engineering and Management Systems. He has published several articles in peer reviewed academic journals and magazines. His writings on lean manufacturing, leadership, productivity, and business appear in Industrial Engineers, Lean Thinking, and Industrial Management. Soliman's blog is www.personal-lean.org.

Also by Mohammed Hamed Ahmed Soliman

https://www.amazon.com/-/e/B00NEY7BRE?fbclid=IwAR1ZM31VKzUyiytw5hKuzu3c9btnuPn08JOb2oA4PWE8h26G_jdG9Cqn2Ag

Recommended reads:

Made in United States
Orlando, FL
17 October 2023

37982822R00041